CW00515459

The Art of Absolution

...

And his shelves housed many books but rarely did he employ them, for like credentials they hung, and rightly so — the trust of many is worth the world in facts

...

Look here upon this society of thespians, cultivated by
reciprocal delusion, matured by observational
amendment. My adolescence pillaged recklessly to state
void of compassion. What is love, if love be irrevocably
blind? This catharsis; this adulterated liberation,
manifestly not blind nor gratifying neither. Alas love
a deficient concept. What is this perpetual adoring,
why this pestilent parasite? A mutual quintessence
presents not. My sterile disposition inept; how can one
adore whilst not adored? What motive is spent upon this
desolate stage? I loathe beauty, I detest company; I
despise what I grasp not. This self-solidarity of
solitude is my narcotic ecstasy in this theatre of
belligerent bastards, this congregation of arrogant
pretentious cretins. What be love but a delusional
comfort? What be life but a dawdling demise? What be
thou, the god; recipient of my vomited discourse? A
nonentity you be but a fictitious token!

CHAPTER ONE

I'll start with suddenly, or just before suddenly, when a thunderous roar rumbled as a thread-like flash of light cracked and shredded the dark canvas that what was prior, a clear sky. Rain plummeted from the heavens like razor-sharp rocks, here I was within this shower of pitchforks, wet, cold, alone, I would have said I was miserable, but sadly that delightful sensation was sadistically waiting in the cafe.

It is a dreary cafe, full of filth, grime, and vulgar characters with as much charm as flat-pack furniture. Arctically cold and callous stubborn plastic chairs perversely riddle the cafe floor like pigeons in Trafalgar Square, whilst a fat ogre like figure of a man attempts to fulfil undesired cravings with the equal passion to that he holds to his own hygiene. The ill-welcoming ambience was swiftly and enigmatically woven under my skin before this ambush by the nicotine-stained grid ceiling as it invades my ever-decreasing space.

The only consolation being granted by that of a nigh transparent window that bestows an almost romantic if feebly depicted depiction of reality. Reality, such an influentially infecting daydream; my body is literally decaying before me and here I am, sitting in a cesspit whilst my intellect is corrupted by the mentally deceased that surrounded me. I've nothing against God personally, but the current splendours of these bio-contraptions and their squalor lie only taint to his credibility.

I ordered an English breakfast. I can't eat it.
I relate to it too much.

$$\sqrt{p} - |\psi\rangle = |-z\rangle \, |+z\rangle$$

...

Even a child with a pocket full of chocolate stars can tell you — nothing is great if something is greater.

...

$$\Delta t' = \Delta t / \sqrt{(1 - v^2/c^2)}$$

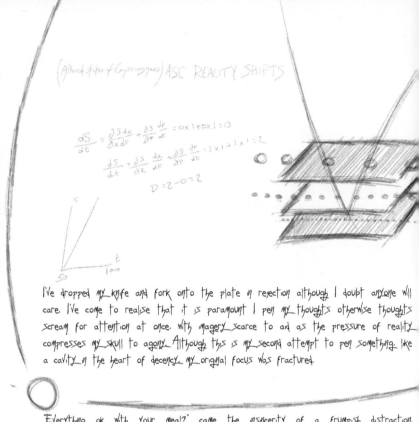

$$\frac{dS}{dt} = \frac{\partial S}{\partial x}\frac{dx}{dt} + \frac{\partial S}{\partial p}\frac{dp}{dt} = 0 \times 1 + 0 \times 1 = 0$$

$$\frac{dS}{dt} = \frac{\partial S}{\partial x}\frac{dx}{dt} + \frac{\partial S}{\partial p}\frac{dp}{dt} = 1 \times 1 + 1 \times 1 = 2$$

$$D = 2 - 0 = 2$$

I've dropped my knife and fork onto the plate in rejection although I doubt anyone will care. I've come to realise that it is paramount I pen my thoughts otherwise thoughts scream for attention at once, with imagery scarce to aid as the pressure of reality compresses my skull to agony. Although this is my second attempt to pen something like a cavity in the heart of decency, my original focus was fractured.

"Everything ok with your meal?" came the insincerity of a frumpish distraction. What a strange enquiry I pondered. Surely it was evident that the platter of coal served does not meet the expectations that a bowl of dripping on a slice of stale bread would have surpassed, and yet there she slumped waiting for a review.

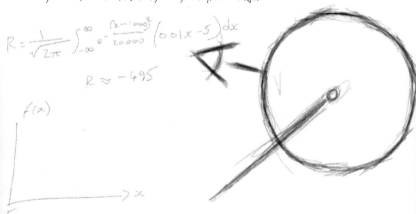

$$R = \frac{1}{\sqrt{2\pi}} \int_{-\infty}^{\infty} e^{-\frac{(x-1000)^2}{20000}} \left(0.01x - 5\right) dx$$

$$R \approx -495$$

But anyway, the attendance of the distraction no more. My attention now on the invading sunlight from the window. It is now sun-drenched outside but a few rain drops darting down the cafe window. One in particular had just caught my interest as it danced like a rugby player dodging across a field before triumphantly crashing to the bottom frame.

Each present state is lost to a past - a trail of water as effect, with only my memory as cause. A motion of a disappearing presence. Past but memory, memory no more tangible reality than a daydream. Calculated only by consequence, only consequence suggesting sequence.

Reality itself nothing but an abstract blob of potential until sustained by the consciousness of life, a collective simulation that weaves a fabric of time and space together to create this mass of mess I see before me.

An apathetic daydream later I now find myself at work. A distribution company_repeatedly_picked ferally_ of value like an abandoned bag of chips left on a pavement. and equally_as infested.

If my_enthusiasm was like toothpaste. then this is really_squeezing and rolling to get the last dregs out.

"Hello!" - sudden obscene outburst of excitement; the kind of candid excitement that only a depressive can craft.

I just can't be like one of them.
Gratefully_wriggling around like maggots in a fisherman's box.

I think there is a girl at work that likes me. I don't know why, I'm trying to not read into it.

When she first spoke to me, she had her hands flat and out from her hips whilst balancing on her toes, seemingly so excited like a Jack escaped from its box.

Conversing with her was the kind of thing I would dream about if one still had the dust in mind to create such fantasy. Like the flick of a light switch to a dark room, she smiled and briefly my body tingled with life once more, like the sensation of pins and needles you get when your blood is rushed back into a dead leg.

Her name is Robyn. When Robyn was five, like many that age she was asked what she wanted to be when she grew up. Little Robyn stood and said proudly and confidently in the face of the laws that bound her that she was going to be a butterfly. Her mind was beautiful like that - such wonders were plausible because the dream was tenacious.

While the rest of us were like moths flying pitifully to the light, she was content in fluttering to the beauty of what the light illuminated.

Her voice is like a hyperactive child acting as a businesswoman but with the sexiness of a sore throat thrown in. To add to her perfection, she has a patience about her, like the deluded optimism of a dreamer combined with the virgin innocence of a child untouched by the world. She feels homely and safe, and is vegan, for she concerns herself with such trivialities as nature, but everybody likes her anyway.

I cherish my time with her; more so because of the depthy murkiness that awaits me in her absence. The last few weeks have passed by in melancholy as my life consists of a smear of leisure time that guts my innate divergence stalked by an occupation that stamped out the remaining floating lit ashes that dance around the corpse of my soul. I don't like being alone; my thoughts are never mine, but instead echoes of a past I have foolishly buried in my mind to escape.

This girl is like something out of a fairy-tale, and what am I? If I were to describe myself, I'd say I looked like a man that was handsome once but had since been hit by a bus. I am the typical failed writer type; cigarette hanging from my red wine-stained lip, scruffy clothed, Ill looking, slouched, an explosion of hair like a motherless child, and as sociable as a mouse trap. But like the sun in the sky shredding the darkness as it raises, in those moments she looks at me, I am the illuminated moon in her passing.

Against a backdrop of black where stars are splat, rivalled in beauty against a moon that's fat. I wonder and drift in mind, as I dance in solitude, blissfully resigned, blissfully renewed.

CHAPTER TWO

Today, relentlessly, Robyn has disclosed further indications that my attention she fancies. There is however a problem to this conclusion; Robyn is not single. Robyn has a partner, Kane, who she also works with. Kane, unfortunately, is a very clever and handsome man, although a little troubled; a trouble which I suspect he uses to justify his cruel and controlling nature; as he pins her butterfly nature to a board. Tied down with surveillance and drowned in suspicion. Robyn has one dream in life - to be a butterfly, and yet apparently every man she has engaged with throughout her life have wanted to pin her down. Such madness is the logic of man, when confronted with such beauty as that of a butterfly, pins it to a board in a desperate act of deluded shared ownership of beauty.

We hugged today, but every clasp breaks with our parting and with an abrupt disorienting crack of the ground beneath my feet, I find myself alone again.

it all started with

"What you writing?"

enquired like the feeble strike of a pickaxe ricocheting off a block of solid ice. it was Carl. accompanied with a resounding expression of sheer bewilderment to the presumably unprecedented act of 'writing'. Carl is the kind of person you almost felt bad for disliking; he would be faultless if not for his thumb-boy appearance — although it suited him.

I'm in the canteen at work. sat on a plastic chair fixed to a table like something you'd expect was designed for a mental hospital. Pale, soulless coloured paint clings to the walls. reflecting the light around the room with an orange tint which compliments the tea-stained cup rings accessorising the tabletops. Redeemably, the room is forgiving in temperature. and silent apart from the humming of a chocolate vending machine and the heavily, exasperatingly lethargic breathing of one Carl, who often opts to sit next to me. His deluded expectation of hospitality is almost charming. before he then begins to forage through his packed lunch that is always so meticulously packed - clearly his wife's work. It was this blundering disturbance that it was brought to my attention the far corner of the canteen. for fashioning a table of their own was Robyn and Kane. appearing hostage to the relatable monotony of elongated trivial pleasantries that is a relationship. Still. I couldn't help but envy.

"Just words" I condescendingly responded to Carl. I didn't like Robyn sitting with Kane. and subsequently I clenched my pen rigidly to the page. almost tearing this paper that lays vulnerable beneath. Carl stuffed his mouth with a fist full of the fugitive lettuce that had escaped his soon to be devoured sandwich.

Why you writing words?" —

I like to strip paper of its virginity, thrusting in my pen and scratching, clawing, ensuring every crevice of its unadulterated skin is exploited. The penetrating ink bleeds within, infecting till the page is ravaged of worth like discarded gift-wrapping left quivering and torn on the floor. Then I expose the next submissive page, vigorously disgracing page after page like a string of insignificant harlots paid and discarded to the back alleys of reality. Until all the beautiful potential that is a blank page is brutally gagged and pillaged like the treacherous daydream that served as my saviour.

"I just like writing." — With little to work with, the dialogue soon discontinued, as did his company once he'd completed nibbling his sandwich down to the crust. Not long after his parting, Kane soon followed to return to work, leaving Robyn and I alone in the canteen.

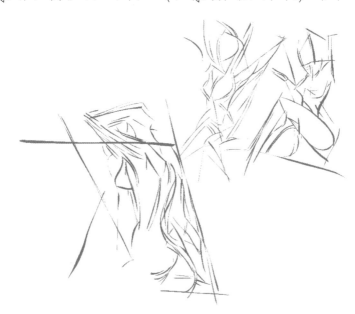

It's a torturing reminiscence on a past of divorced reactions, awakening surging regret that beams reflections in fractions. Neither follow nor play in this mystical movement; yet a cross of fear wavers doubts to my impending judgement. With believed hostility aside along with my loathing of those blind. I am in-part apprehensive of what His jury will find?

What followed was such a confusing interaction.

"OK?" she sparked as she approached my table with a cautious smile dragged with awkwardness: like with her every step that brought her.

"You OK?" I replied with a forced joy whilst forcibly stuffing my notebook back into my pocket, perhaps emphasising desperately my appetite for her engagement.

"We OK?" she retorted as she took seat, arms crossed for comfort and shoulders protruding towards me attentively. I loved her looking at me: it sent such an erotic quiver through my body. She looked with such sincerity and focus, with total disregard of all external concerns. I knew for them precious moments: she was all mine.

"Why wouldn't we be?" I enquired but she paused silent, like waiting a punch line to a joke of ambiguous ethics.

"I've never been better" I leaned back to stretch, physically and mentally, my stolen facility for life, for love, returned. A feeling of potential was stitching the rugged corners of the falsely-apparent trivial messiness in place, as all lingering residue of solitude lining my stomach was deliquescing, the putrefied froth of an obligatory being washed away like a cry torn and shredded by the cut-throat howling of the wind.

Alas, the conversation ostensibly curdled, silence fell on the table, even the ticking of her wristwatch cowered away. It was the kind of awkward silence not seen between us since we first began to converse. Her transitory celebration was patently testimony to an unspoken woe. I didn't know what was clouding her sight, but I took reassurance with the assumption that her prior conversation with Kane was the cause.

I can't stop thinking about her. Such faultless modesty — she could wither a rose with its own envy.

I spoke to her again today in the canteen. But as she spoke, I was just riveted by her animated lips as they danced with such erotic and arbitrary passion. I didn't even hear a word she was saying. Her lips moved and I was lost in a trance, tranquilized with admiration. As these days pass, I have become more and more obsessed, even in absence from presence she clouded my psyche.

Now you could speak of the delicate random perfections of snowflakes like some church choir schoolboy lying in bed with his boxing gloves on — but she is the blizzard that is tearing new dimensions as she bridges the gap between fantasy and reality. The creation of the world is an insult to complexity compared to her. She distorts my sense of time and warps my concept of space. She is the piercing light of a sunrise slashing and slaughtering its way through the darkness of night. Shadows flee and hide around every corner from where she stands. She is the rhythm in my heart — the very quintessence of every pulse that tears its way through it. Every second away from her drives me mad. My very breath is denied — as more and more my heart aches with every pathetic and wasted beat it musters in her absence, relinquishing its instinct as it drowns in its own blood, devoured by life. I've become a discarded book, left open and abandoned on the floor, as the wind flicks through my pages from start to finish, washing away every rational grasp - every anchor on reality I hold in footnote.

When your meaning lies in another, you become a husk without them, and it angers you, as you yell at every reflectional repel. Everything becomes a side-tracked wondering that becomes your pondering. Meaning destroyed, madness employed, with just a whistle of a name, and you become the philosopher in a godless world demanding an answer from the void in which you came!

What now? What now? As she continued to speak words that never survived the journey to my ears - I am falling in love with her.

If it could, it would, for it should suffice to say my immortal worry was suppressed eventually by the palpable property of present. It should, alas, as always - it is not, in a world of silhouettes and misinterpretations, it remains man's greatest vice. Why would not it be so? The world is nothing if not a translation we fashion, but in the form of a hope too imperative to suffocate there is always that whisker of opposition — that seedling of hope, like the human instinct to sustain your own existence despite all the opposing logic of the brain. This was the foreplay of love - pieces are forming to place and I am petrified.

"Tell me something nice about *you*" she asked — I momentarily panicked - my head was not normally home to 'nice' guests. I dug deep: I'd already blocked out most of my high school years and nothing interesting had happened to me since.

I told her about how when I was little, in primary school, I was asked to write a Christmas letter to Santa. I said I wanted a spaceship, but not a rocket, because I didn't just want to go there, I wanted to live there. I tried to draw the one from Star Trek to make sure he got the right idea, but I couldn't draw it. So, I drew a cat instead because I knew how to draw cats. She laughed with fondness —

She told me that I was special, and that I had beautiful eyes that look at her like how no one has ever looked at her before. Now I've read enough romance novels to know that this is the moment I kiss her, my head was screaming it. I said how my eyes only appeared beautiful because they were looking at her, but my mind was just screaming to shut up and kiss her.

This is how it happened, nearly every day, every hour, minute, every second I was with her. Kiss her! Kiss her! But I never did. Frustratingly I'd let her slip away every single time. All that light which her presence brought, the raging heat, like a fire roaring in a towering inferno of dancing demons that blinded me with retina burn, the labyrinths of majestic vivid rays of erotic ember that danced passionately around us in a symphony of lust as all the colliding energy of two untameable beasts of desire clashed in uniform, ripping, tearing, would vapour, nothing.

For soon, as always, the moment would pass and returns nothing but a reminiscing over a spark of flint from a broken lighter - she walked away from my grip.

But I wasn't letting that happen this time. I moved toward her. She moved toward me. I could tell in her breath as it whispered in release. She knew the plot. She knew what was coming. as the warm fingers of her hand gripped mine. We stared. fixated on each other's eyes for what seemed the turn of a century_ barely_a blink in break. expression frozen in relax. mind awash of a thousand thoughts. not one present. It was going to happen: I was going to kiss her. The tips of her lips opened ajar as she closed her eyes. even the curves of her cheekbones erotically_inviting me like a Venus flytrap to a blundering fly. The furious thrill of rushing blood in my twitching body of veins throbbed my_excitement like a fire alarm in the back of my_electrified eyes as

my_breath quivered with ecstasy_But then. as soon as I felt her breath upon

me. followed by her lips tickling and teasing the tips of mine. savouring the stimulation of pleasure galore. a harmonious moment of complete stillness was presented in pause. complete unity_and complete completeness fell. Like my whole
life was to build to this moment. this perfect moment. the clocks stopped. the

Earth stopped. the very_beating of my_heart stopped. And as the heavy_ weight of a void of voidness fell upon me. crushing. like a bucket of ice water.

my_last breath was stolen - and in theft. we kissed.

The lapse of the pulse remains irrepressible with blackness melded and shades inexpressible. The infinite infinite compressed into nought and measured by that of sight and thought. Hours, years, and centuries all rhyme — it's the rhythm of life, the rhythm of time.

CHAPTER TWO AND A HALF

I detest mirrors; my incarcerated body staring back at me. The unreflected me - the mind is external, with spiritual potential that's infinitely eternal. I have no limits, neither beginnings nor ends. I encompass all, and all thereafter. 'I' is total, absolute, and is unconditionally everything and all thereafter — the spaces in-between are an effect to a cause to which I play no conscious part. I have no name for I occupy no form of boundary in any form of dimension. However, a trivial glance to a mirror and I'm stubbornly distinguished by the surroundings and confined to a piercing straight sharp strident line, webbed forcibly into reality and imprisoned by time.

The most heartless and cruel curse is not to be trapped, but to know that you're trapped. I need to escape this restriction, this binding, this space, this time. I've been studying time for so long now that my notebook is almost full, and all that studied time has done is waste what time I have. My short-rationed supply of time has been folded and slotted between a bounding of leather, it takes time to escape time, and I've simply not the time. The foremost concern with being alive is the supplementary side effect of death, and nothing in comparison can highlight quite as prominent and subtle my looming death as that of my own reflection.

It is always there, death, whilst I am dancing in ignorance, it is there. I can feel its presence, like a reality I am ignoring, just ticking away in the background. Like my corpse is just right there, all this time, under the floorboards below where I stand, waiting patiently.

We had a date. I know conventionally I was to take a lady to a dance, a meal, or for coffee. However, I had neither the skill to dance nor the charm to dine, so I opted for a quiet pub and countered my lack of charm with a pack of playing cards. The pub was comfortably homely in its welcome. Tables thick of oak and wooden chairs worn encouragingly into comfort with age. Maroon reds and pine greens generously veiled the walls and bar whilst dim lights littered the ceiling like stars under the trivial clinking of glasses nibbling in the distance. Small groups of friends charmingly nattered gently like little pods of peas, favourably isolating our own presence romantically. I'd tried to comb my hair, and I even fashioned a shirt, it was missing cuff buttons, but it was the only one I owned. As for Robyn, she'd gone for a classically smart black dress that hugged her angel-carved figure whilst cultured trinkets tastefully and modestly decorated her naturally - and refreshingly. I was used to girls wearing jewellery like Christmas trees wear baubles.

She was beautiful, and perfect, and the class difference was as evident as my missing buttons. But she never stopped smiling, and neither did I as I began to feel what I always imagined being normal felt like — I belonged.

The raw virgin cards were dealt playfully onto the table as I counted the given hands, our eyes catching a glance quickly becoming a stare, and with every hookerish flick of a card being placed to the table her gaze turned more and more narrow and fixated on me. I grew cocky with every minor victory I played forth - she responded frustrated, like a tense holding of aggravation, furthered still by the arduous irritation that whilst she was annoyed by my victory, my vaunt, and annoyed further by my flamboyantly presumptuous forecast of further triumph, she was visibly tortured by the incontrovertible truth that despite my conceited superiority, she, right then, there in that pub, as she clenched her cards in her fist, squinting her eyes and biting her lips shut, had never "wanted" me so much! Her face was losing battle to remain poker faced, so naturally I played on this like the plucking of a restrained guitar string. Never had a deal of a card been so charitable in my favour, as I continued to be undeservingly victorious, and she continued vexed, violent and as passionate as a strike of a violin string, the overwhelming desire: a devilishly craving of ravenous need: a sordid thrust of lust, as rapist thoughts clawed her rationality, leaving her nigh quivering and short of breath, as every dire pant became a traitorous teasing releasing steadily a flood flushing and crushing her down to a core of animalistic desire, want, and need, to rip, to claw, to take.

Time skipped a passing and tailored a jump. That night I found myself naked and willingly restrained to a bed by her hands. She with a devilish expression of feral curiosity, almost vacantly clouded with want, like a starved cave girl, squatted over her pray. Such wildness would warrant fear had one's emotional stability not been equally pulverized, as every thorn-laced throb of blood choked all deviating thought in murder. She releases me from my restraining as her quivering fingers mischievously waltzed slowly down my body with every exploratory circling teasing me. She moved in towards me. I felt her breath tickle the fine hairs of my neck as she moved slowly up to my ears. I clenched her hips: the digging of my nails excited her as her brief quivers of breath intensified in my ears. She nibbled downwards along my neck as I clawed my nails up her back and spine. Suddenly she grabbed my shoulders as she pulled herself toward my ears again, whispering filthily in dire hunger. "fuck me"...

Do you know what passion is? It's not some hippy love festival of flowers, dancing, making daisy chains and those cute little notes you leave around the house reminding your partner how romantic you can be. Passion is fire, it's desperation: it's a clawing in your throat right down to your heart, like a gritty belligerent need for life when you're already alive! An imploding tapping, like a clock that's rapping in the hunger of a silent scream, scratching, clawing, massacring every now tainted enclosure.

I had never had sex like that before and judging by the gratefully damaged look in her eyes, she'd never either.

CHAPTER FOUR

Notebook, pages fall — burdening ink — pages drink — like of blood as fibres link — words over words over words they sink. Vandalising every charge of reason, in a game of logical treason, like just another, and another, and another curve round a curve of never-ending curves. Temporal contractions, time in fractions, layers of reactions, pluses and subtractions, a pulse of present, and past, and future. A theory of B theory of a wiggly stringy spiralling thingy that goes round and round and round in a straight line! Tick tock tick tock ticky tocky fucking swinging pendulum, death! Clock! An abundancy of inconsistencies, they mock, screaming for assimilation, answers, theories, a man of many men infesting the head. Sense they gnaw, more and more! To whom listen? To whom me?

There is no feasible closure. time is cause; to travel it is to slow down your relation in transition. I can't win. all I can do is lengthen what inhabits no length. The knot slips but the rope shortens!

"The hot water tap in the men's toilets are playing up again."

Your brain is like a computer - a web of reactions, thoughts and choices mapped like a set of algorithms overlaying further sets of algorithms you've forged in learning.

"So now you've got to go from the toilets to the canteen just to wash your hands."

For each new challenge is countered by transferable algorithms you modify, with further algorithms. Where is she?

"The whole thing seems a little unsanitary to me."

The brain, therefore, and all its reactions and seemingly spontaneous fancies, are so much predictable that the predictable becomes the predetermined.

"Personally, I've just been using the cleaner's sink next door."

Time itself becomes not a line of events but a dot, all the way back to the time of when the universe was the size of a pea. For everything is connected. every quantum sized quiver sends waves of disturbance throughout the matter of that what surrounds me. Why is she not here already?

"Are you OK?" interrupted Carl. It was quarter-past twelve, and there was still no sign of Robyn. my sanity was now source to a grave buckle under which the burden of inkling lay. An alteration of heart. Kane. or death. Each almost humorously immorally equal in measure of severity.

It is not a fear that I could die if she disappeared. I once prided myself on my abbreviated life - It was the realisation that I was always dead anyway. like my time with her was nothing but the skimming of a gritty rock across the rippling surface of water.

I SAID I'M FINE, I WASN'T.

I finally seen Robyn again today. She entered the canteen with a new haircut. So much shorter than usual, she looked almost punkish. She sat mournfully, anxiety and nausea layering her face like a veil. I waited an explanation but following a pause of silence I enquired in concern.

"I need a place to live" She surrendered with a tone of anger like I should have already known. She continued to stroke sorrowfully the ripples of plastic down the cup of water I had supplied her in waiting — staring lost into a void that clearly lay before her and the world. Now as horrid as a man I may be. and I'd agree. but the news did inject such immeasurable joy in me, as I wished distance between her and Kane to be as bitterly great as possible. but due to the expression of joy being. I felt, inappropriate. I resided and compromised with a reflection of concern. I knew he was only throwing her out so that she'd beg her way back. I didn't trust him as far as I could throw him, and with him being over a foot taller than me. the use of the word 'far' was somewhat in itself. mere flattery to my own ability.

I detest Kane. Waiting for her like a claw-legged spider in the corner of a sinister web, as I drifted into the night with nothing for companionship but my own paranoia. I'd see him sometimes, a smear of hatred in the window reflection. watching me. Kane! With his socks that match. a job that he actually chose to do. hair combed with an actual comb and not just his fingers. and a man's chin. a real chin. one of those you could scoop ice cream with. What do I have? A pair of shoes that had the soles glued on and a watch that I wore despite the flat battery that died several months before.

Visions torment me - him climbing into her bed at night whilst she slept, touching her against her will, and with greater fear was the horrid reality that hurting her in force was not something below his known standards. With her absence in greater value, rationality would abandon. All trace of reason is swept away with the chilling breeze of what if: concepts of her willingly playing part in their potential activities taunt me fluently like the foreplay of a demon. It may not have even been Kane - she liked attention. When she was little, if ignored, she would lay herself across the doorway - the bitter transition from child to adult that normally hits us like a steel mallet to the head did nothing but lick her disposition. She may no longer arrange herself across the doorway now, but her principles were the same. What charmer could make her stray? What creep could weasel her away?

Paranoia! Such a powerful word to mutter let used for the most perilous of thoughts. Lingering fancies pluck each notion in my mind, like a puppeteer stirring a concoction of jealousy to which what was left of me became a mere feature. Perhaps, of course, maybe, without a doubt, it's possibly probable that while these primitive men may strive to be civilised, woman may in-between civility fancy a flex of muscle to ensure her mate's adequacy. Or maybe, perhaps, probably something an ex had constructed to build me up before knocking me down in some devilish scheme. I didn't know what to believe, but you can justify anything if you have enough time, and in the play of her absence, I have plenty.

I told Robyn she should come live with me. She replied 'OK', hesitantly — and so short a response - it troubles me: I could not decipher her desire but greedily favoured her ill-committed submission, and now she is here. We are living together now, which is great. But I can't help but feel something isn't right. This is all happening really fast I know, but it is like this is in a manner like we had done so for some time now. It's hard to explain, but it doesn't feel like she has 'moved in' but rather that she has simply just 'come back'.

CHAPTER FIVE

Bulbous mocking playground maggots now swim in the pus of the festered blisters they formed. The lugubrious cries of a falsely glorified foetus feed their curious fetish. My skin stretched, clawing away the smeared mucus to get a tear, "Hey! He's retarded in there" – They squirt, they phlegm, a gesturing secretion, for those that don't compare – and the little fuckers are everywhere!

It all starts with a look, the
tale of the wizard of
sensations. If you hid in your
knee and put the words. You're
letting out the emotional
extravaganza that is the
quintessence of life. An artist
will twist a tale with a delicate
turn of a tip and a pinch of
cheese. The tale becomes
lost in the transition but then
the paper contently feeds on
the emotional afterbirth

I found myself in an abandoned school playground: my old school playground to be precise. In the centre stood a door, just a door, no walls, no room, just a large wooden door. It was raining. Countless children's faces watched me from the windows of the school. I opened the door; but creaks portrayed a door not opened for a very long time and revealed was nothing but darkness. Only with the flash of lightning from behind me did the true distance of the hall unveil itself. A series of dead dried up plants housed in oversized pots cut lengthy distorted shadows across the unadorned walls. There was a stale dampness in the whispering air that shivered my spine and moistened my palms. To the far right-hand side of the hallway however came something curious – with every flash of lightning this far wall remained seductively in darkness. I moved slowly towards the wall on my right. I floated my fingers over the light switch, debating whether I truly desired to know what waited in the corner. The ominous atmosphere turned electric, the hairs on my arms and the back of my neck erected in fright. The eerie isolated confusion excited me.

The foreboding silence screamed in my ears. I inhaled deeply and flicked the switch. On flared the light bulb with an echoing ping. Nothing there: not a thing! Only as I turned to leave did I notice I wasn't alone: there was a small boy cowardly curled up in the corner behind the door. To my accepting disbelief, the boy was clearly me as a child, dressed in the same ghastly cardigan that my mother would dress me in.

A releasing thrill of madness befell me as I seized an oversized plant pot and proceeded to strike it over the boy's skull, over and over again. An energetic flash of ecstasy excited every vein in my body with each crack and crushing of his collapsing skull. I laughed hysterically as my eyes were electrified by the sight of his skull cracking like an eggshell. He didn't even put up a fight: his limp and lifeless body burdened no more by a retarded, rejected, pathetic lump of unlovable shit!

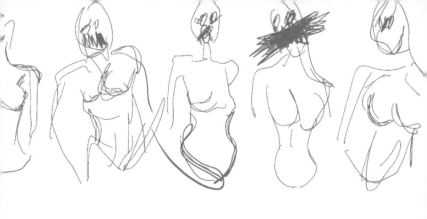

I breathe in. I breathe out. every_focus focused on the focus to lose the very_focus I'm focusing. I breathe in. I breathe out. That silence - after every_tick, before every_tock. when even the weight of silence has lifted. and the anchor of gravity_drifted. I breathe in. I breathe out. A defiance - shifted. A chain. a clink. a link. in a blink. of a thinketh. a breve. I breathe. out. I breathed. out.

I was trapped in limited shades of disfigurement, layered on layers of layers, spiralling through an existential daydream where neither I nor he nor they formed anything other than treason to reason.

...to feel a comfort in discomfort.

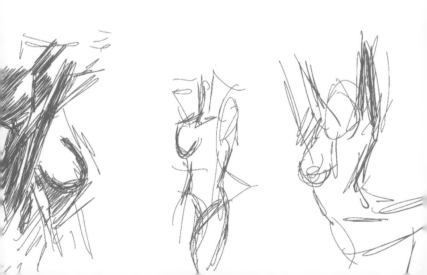

CHAPTER SIX

I encompass deeply a memory — a memory of blocking out a memory from a time I no longer hold as my own. Robyn would ask frequently to what this memory was. She'd say she could see a trouble in my eyes, but I couldn't tell her. For once said memories are discussed, they are shared. Once shared they cannot be killed. It's a memory buried so deep within myself that just reminiscing over the blocking alone pulverises my heart with every palpitation. It is unstable, a potential so terrifying to my existence that my own self-preservation dislocates me.

Things happened to me: a lot of things happened to me that caused me to detach myself from myself. I reinvented myself. I cut off all ties to my past. I dealt with unsaid memories by placing them in myself, killing myself mentally and being reborn as a new. These memories now lie with a child to which I hold no association: a vile and putrid child whose existence I care not to entertain. That child is dead, and if he weren't, I would kill him myself.

No action is chosen, they are but results from experiences that were also the product of previous experiences of them that dictate mine. Whilst adversary to contentment as it pillages self-worth, ego feeds on the entitlement I encased in hope. Despite conflicted with a moral compass I constructed in humour, judge how one is judged I do judge. I assume the probable intellect as measurement to reasoning, that is conceived on a reflection of a set to which they fall. Can I be blamed for the stability of said reflection if data presented not, I am with irregularities? Admittedly verdict may lean towards that likely to be disapproved by the subject in judgement, but of course my favour will be in their unfavourable favouring for favoured I never was. I was judged so little that little I became. So forgive me if my judgments are a little harsh whilst I suffer to this day a menial job, surrounded by the shadows of them that are but of little else. Trapped, contained, in a small box stored in their memories to which I still exist. For so long as they hold a memory of my inferiority, then inferior will be all that I am, all that I see in the mirror every day of my life.

Man will fritter his grievances in a delusional compromise that we are what we make ourselves, however, as unfortunate as it may appear to them at the bottom, you are what the world makes you. In much the way that a tea pot will never be prime minister, it is generally more palatable for all parties involved if the tea pot is the one to blame.

I found myself in my hallway, rickety slabs of sound scratched like steel icebergs screaming in a sluggish collision. The hallway led to a door, open ajar, teasing a trouble I cared not to learn. But still I was drawn, I was pulled, I was enchanted. I crept through the door, my body withdrawn in defence from a room that was awkward and disturbed. The wallpaper was distraught by colour, and patterns disowned by coherency. Dust coated cobwebs riddled the dim light that hung from the ceiling, still swinging from a now absent breeze, bringing every shadow in the room to an unwelcoming life. The floor lay bare to tell of time and housed a reflection from the window.

The window, oh the window. A horrid window of evil; of dismay that I still witness as I write. The window that looked out to a sea of faces, yes faces, hideous long tormented faces. Grey - a kind a grey that even a mad artist wouldn't play with. A grey that colours would never dare combine. A grey of a death still choking on a cord of enough life to whim a heartbeat so painfully pounded that it would steal each beat of mine. The faces' features were almost swollen like they were victim to a watery grave - each one expressed a story, a moan of a torture which had lasted an eternity. Each face watching, like a warning to a fate I had no path back from.

The most devilishly torturous part, more sickening to my stomach, more overwhelming than their unsolicited presence; they were not a welcoming party to my fate. They were not even there for me, like a nightmare within a nightmare of nightmares as an inner quiver of realisation violently shredded me from within upon stolen breath.

I realised that they were not looking at me. Over a thousand eyes burrowed their focus into this room that I was within, and yet not one single eye was on me. They were looking behind me - every single eye from every single corpse was utterly fixated on one thing, and that thing had put the horror into the eyes of horror. Whatever this thing was, was in the kitchen, just behind me. I turned - I didn't want to. Believe me of all my many wishes at that moment, this wish was not mine. But I turned. I turned to see what was so horrid, so evil, that evil itself observed with caution, with fascination. I turned: I turned to this boundless evil, sweat coating me in a shiver, my eyes stinging with fear. I turned. Every hair on my body erected by the electric scream of a screaming unheard. I turned, my heart ripping itself from my chest. I turned, my breath suffocating, lungs devouring themselves, my hands, my body — also clutched in a moment of cannibalism. I turned, my nails digging into my palms - a pain I noticed but did not feel. I turned. I turned...

I TURNED

I then woke up. I woke up alone. Robyn was gone. I was in what had become an oversized bed and she was not accounted for. I couldn't even relish in her distant warmth that would often remain on her side of the bed for evidently she had been absent for some time. I stumbled from my slumber and succumbed myself to the calling of a significance that even nightmares refused to entertain. Presently insignificant I grant you — but I promise you, within this insignificancy lays the unspeakable truth to this whole tale of fiendish deception. The insignificancy was a glass of water. Upon the departure from my bed I noticed a glass, tipped and empty. The carpet was wet but the water hadn't yet soaked in, like the gates of hell themselves refused its entry. I pondered it trivially before leaving the room.

I could hear nothing but the hiccupping gargle of birdsong echoing through an abyss of silence. I could see the dust adrift in the air, sparkling like a collective massacre of stars, dancing in the sunlight that bled through a crack in the curtain before drifting down through the bitterly tainted and derelict air, never landing, for land lay home to an unspeakable injustice.

There lay the end of the world, the point in which time itself will not pass, where the whole of the universe and everything in it, where everything that ever was and could have been, every feeling, every thought, every spark of love and hope, every given tear and shiver of fear, from the Big Bang and that millisecond of infinity before it, every evolutionary triumph of determination and adaptation, every struggle, every success, everything, now nothing more than a full stop - a little black dot at the end of a story that had now lost its' story. Alone without a past nor future, like the birth and death of a star. Everything gone. Everything I was, everything I am. I have become as dead as the cold colourless corpse of Robyn that then lay before me.

CHAPTER SIX AND A HALF

Breadcrumbs, breadcrumbs - dust of time, floats down a river of a watery_rhyme. Notebook becomes notebooks, to cover each crime — but everywhere breadcrumbs — dust of time. Manufactured lines point to gathered declines, spiralling in a straight line of lines of lines to a time of times, fractured times — the dust, you miss, like the rust from distrust, like a kiss of an abyss you dismiss, with every_twist and every_twine, scatters of matters, - dust of time. Memories — times' treasures - enemies to energies flow in chains of tomorrow's yesterdays. It's a craze - this maze of many_exiting ways, a phrase of days but my_mind strays, in a fixated daze of choice, ablaze of relays, voice over voice over voice — my_days of no days, my_way_of no ways, with my_sanity in paraphrase, time I travelled — sideways. In a room of insignificance did crumble a torture, where a latter became neither latter nor former, my_body_felt deformed and terribly_mistaken, as time was reformed and forever forsaken. Internally_I screamed a formidable fiend: a quarantined suspicion that this was all schemed. Matched to rival my_nails frantically_fed, sensations lay_idle whilst my_fingers bleed. My_skin felt tight but permissively_restrictive, even as I write, the numbness, it's addictive — in misery_I gorged, I'd never felt so unforged. I slipped through a non-present gap to a place non-present on a map. A compilation of years had passed, a timeline of history_ amassed. As spirals of darkness surrounded me, I could see the universe the size of a pea, all the energies linking like the roots of a tree, a reversal big_bang, before dispersing free. That is what it is, that is what we all are, a collection of spirals, all floated too far. A white noise infected - sense of compression, only_faltering to a turn of gears, each a deliverance of confession. An implausible spectrum of colour flooded my_vision, with shadows torn in a display_of collision, a cut of precision, to contrast division, history's emission, through a God's delinquent commission. There came an objection to direction, a time path rejection, and in so I accepted myth. It was astral projection - this resurrection - that danced its potential forthwith. I saw my_life expunged, in my_mind my_sanity_plunged. When time consumes a past of regret, built of unprofitable debt, like a blank cassette, a wanted forget, a willed surrogate — you accept. I didn't understand why, but I was happy_to lie, it was this indulgence or die.

All of space and time is balanced on a rhythm of lemons and lime, a puppet-master's elusive rhyme, of a precarious design, now ponders from the bottle of cheap red wine.

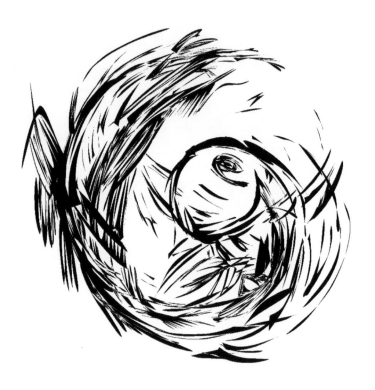

And like the trivial yank of a chain, flush, the fish now dead to her, like it meant nothing to her.

You're spinning now, around, and around, aimlessly within the basin of the toilet. You look up, to see her one last time, but she's already gone, she's at the pet store now, replacing you.

And you come out the other end, a life without her. But you're out of water now, left gasping for air, jump, jump, but now you jump no more, slowly gasping now, then gasping less and less as the realisation settles in on top of where your dwindled hope last stood, she's gone, she has actually gone this time, and she isn't coming back.

You gasp your last gasp, but what's the point? You let go now. Your glazed eyes staring ahead but not focused on a thing, for her face you can't see now, you see nothing now, for nothing now is there.

CHAPTER THREE

A rage, a scrap, to win, to lie, to cage, to trap, to pin, to tie.
A gutter, a slap, a black eye! No flutter, no flap, a dead butterfly...

Every breath starts after your last.

A nice house accompanied by many identical houses - with windows of modern sufficiency and a door of equal measure. Flowers of many pointless bloomings littered their fruitless pleasantries across a garden that bordered. Inside lay a collection of decorous furniture to compliment the notion of no concern, conceited ornamental gatherings of meaninglessness paid tribute. A house so crammed with joyfully impertinent trivialities, the perfect portrayal of perfection was projected, the perfect lie.

Robyn once resided here with her partner Kane, and the outside world saw only the scatters of truth that he sewed together. His troubles became the threads that stitched the fabrics of violence to make a blanket of a lie that cloaked them — and to the world it looked beautiful.

It was here in the settling mist of a morning, through slithers of loose threads did spark a suspicion. Robyn woke that day to find Kane standing over her, a letter in fist, and a glare of a dare that even a God would choose forfeit. With the letter as decoy, soon a second fist exposed the fancy to a knife that he held, and with several stabs and slashings, the bedding was slaughtered beneath her laying from which she fled. His eyes flickering with rejection as every unjustified attack he had burdened her prior was now, in his eyes, justified. A rib or three, a broken jaw, a fractured arm, it didn't really matter. Robyn would forgive them all, for in his past lay further horrors. He would apologise, and they would hug and say "never again".

It had almost become the routine, the expected, the accepted, that each week ended, with Kane dropping a fist or two unintentionally intended. He would often find himself in a knot of suspicion, which he had tied with a fabricated fiction. But this time was new, he had a letter to hold, this fashioned a captive, in a fist shaped mould. No apology was waiting, only a path to an end, to which she could no longer defend.

"You fucking slag!" he said whilst towering over her, she cowered to the floor by the sink in the kitchen to which she had now fled. Mercifully he then surrendered the knife to gravity and walked out the door. As Robyn heard the front door being locked, she accepted whatever fate that would necessitate the locking out of the world. After all, this was her world, that once small girl that dreamt of being a butterfly — the symbol of freedom, now owned and pinned by what she had learned and been trained to accept as her fault.

Then, like the flick of a switch to a room that had been victim to darkness for so long, life had been granted by her own conscious as the sound of his car driving away brought a flood of salvation to her ears - he hadn't locked them in, he had locked her in. I guess a fear had always trapped her, but it was an acceptance that sealed her.

CHAPTER ONE AND A HALF

'Eww! It looked at me' giggled a small group of girls that floated by

amongst the sea of faceless children that flooded down the school corridors.

The boy looked to the floor, there his feet housed by a pair of shoes,

two sizes too small.

A reek of mould oozed from every abandoned moist towel that besieged the lengthy slender wooden benches that ran parallel across the room like slashes across a virgin wrist. Like from a noose hung bulging gym bags that anchored from hooks that stalked the stretch of benches from above like vultures hunched. They guided a way to a narrow slit in the walls that led to the school's shower area. Every inch of wall gave residence to a residue of scum coated tiles that offered no offering of grip, surrounding numerous discoloured shower heads that towered over a nest of clogged grids.

'Well? What are you waiting for?' shouted the teacher, as he casted his shadow over a runt of a boy, quivering with nerves, quivering with shame, like a lamb in a dungeon of dragons. 'Take off your clothes then! You have to be naked to get a shower – you stupid spastic!' Every boy – now dressed – waiting with a sneer and with sheer anticipation in pre-gratification, almost rocking on their bums, like the waiting of a public execution.

The boy slowly undressed, each exposed body part enriching the amusement of his audience. The teacher laughed so hard that tears spewed from his close-set eyes, as children exaggerated their laughs in loyalty by lead with emphasis on his shame. "Look everybody — look at this skinny spastic!"

It was never enough for people to believe him stupid; satisfaction was never met until they'd beaten him down with it. The laughing flooded his senses and choked him as he felt the hands of a boy push him over onto the cold hard floor. This never stopped — this was his life — forever the joke, the runt, the pointless point whose point in life was to make other people feel better about themselves...

Beautifully sinister curtains drifted into animation with each phantom breeze that donated a splinter of moonlight in a seductive tease of illumination. Shivering shadows waltzed on their toes across the sharp forms of the room. Each form of surface bringing birth to alternative forms of light that sparkled like stars reflected of a lake. The beauty of this seclusion laid tinted only by the dishonesty that befell a corner in constant discomfort. There came the sobbing of a small boy slumped. Upon further focus soon came the submission of dismay, why the shadows dared not cross path with the murkiness of the distress. For hidden from the reality in denial was a boy tearing out lump by lump his own internal organs. With a sobbing that indicated not despair, but despair in lacking of, as each meaningless organ greeted the floor with such casual insignificance.

He stopped sobbing to turn and look at me, a pause that granted his hollow eyes the power to paralyse me in fear. He then screamed a scream that only an animal could rally, so emotionally raw in emotionless emotion, it burrowed within my reflexes, impregnating me with a comfort undisclosed to logic — he was me — he was always me - everything was me.

My name is irrelevant, it always has been, never noticed, never seen.

Because I believed them, I believed them all. I built a dreamland: a haven. I built a wall. I developed a hunch because I looked to the

floor —

there lay all my hopes and dreams, there lay nothing more.

I WAKE FROM A SLEEP I NEVER HAVE BUT NEVER LEAVE, SURROUNDED BY GODS IN WHICH I DON'T BELIEVE, AS EVERYTHING I DO WAS WHAT I DID IN DENIAL, AND EVERYTHING I DID I WILL DO ON TRIAL. I WAKE FROM A SLEEP I NEVER HAVE BUT NEVER LEAVE, SURROUNDED BY A CONSCIENCE ONLY I CONCEIVE. AS MY HOURGLASS LAYS SMASHED UPON A FLOOR OF FROST, I AM COLD, I AM LONELY, AND I AM LOST.

CHAPTER SEVEN

"Please don't kill me" he squirmed pathetically like a spineless worm as he begged on his knees before the gun I held to his head. I presented him with a plastic cup: his vacant look of confusion thrilled me.

"If you want to live then piss into this cup!" He looked at the plastic cup and paused momentarily before proceeding to carry out my request. Kane already looked beaten, but I hadn't finished. I took great pleasure, great, great pleasure as I looked down on him kneeling before me, broken, with a cup of warm piss in his hand.

"My taxi is due in a minute" sparked Robyn whilst she got ready — preparing her eyelashes with precision; mouth wide open, staring into the mirror, as I sat daydreaming into my own palms, phasing from one reality to another.

"Now drink it" I commanded. Kane gave no further thought and began to drink what he could in-between each whimpering quiver of repulsion. As he cowered there, shivering with fear, I had so many sensations travelling though my body that I failed to pin a single one down. But I felt dark, and powerful, like the wrath of a deity was flowing through me. He then finished and looked up to me in waiting as I concluded - 'You don't know me, and you'll never find me - but know this: right here, right now, I own you. I own every inch of you, and I will leave you here with a smile on my smug undeserving face in that knowing, and every time from now on when you look at your pathetic self in the mirror, vision this moment, vision my face, when you belonged to me, and above all, remember that I am better than you!"

"Are you sure you don't mind me going out?" — She paused seeking reassurance, with an expression of sincerity clashed with a stance of frustration; she was still used to being in a trapped relationship where she wasn't allowed to go out with her friends. I always promised myself that I wouldn't trap her like Kane did — I never understood why he did.
"Of course, I don't mind" I replied, I smiled.

She was so intriguingly innocent looking in her apparent disposition by the mere flutter of her movements, and a town in dusk - perilous in witness to such fluttering flutters. But I can't be like Kane — I can't trap her even if it was the best thing for her. She would be out all night, sometimes into the dawn of the next, and when she returned, she was as distant as she was when she was away. I'd spend the night alone at my desk, repeatedly doodling the figure of eight on the cover of my notebook.

I had broken time; I was in and out of moments like blots of ink on water, floating, stretched, and dragged by the very currents that supported me — I lay, as I witnessed the life of a dead girl living.

I wasn't me: I was encased and bound in stretched threads like layers of coarse cloth that I fashioned as skin. My fingernails felt so desiccated and brittle that they mimicked a sensation of detachment. I could feel the greased-up bone within my fingers slither under the jelly of fat that layered beneath my skin.

I could feel the slow onion-like crunching of my eyes with every blink as my ears amplified the nothingness of the air around me, like a delusion of reality was lifting. My muscles felt reduced to a cord, like a rope, fraying, tearing. My stomach felt to collapse open, like I'd been gutted alive — I could almost feel the wetness where my entrails had slivered out, almost hearing the nigh crackling of infinitesimal frail fibres as the blood bled into the fabric cloth of my skin.

My stomach was my opening, my escape from this vile corpse in which my mind had been trapped. I could vision myself rip open further away the skin, through the membrane, and cracking, like an eggshell, inverting myself — freeing myself.

Please don't kill me" he squirmed pathetically like a spineless worm as he begged on his knees to the gun I held to his head. I presented him with a plastic cup: I then proceeded to unzip my trousers, as his look of concern amused me. I began to piss into the cup, with aim of little interest — there was a surprising amount still left for him to hold. I imagined the warmth of my piss in his hands, it pleased me. Kane already looked beaten but I hadn't finished. An imposing contentment contained me, as I looked down to him grovelling before me, defeated, with a cup of warm piss in his hand.

"My taxi is due in a minute" sparked Robyn whilst she got ready — mouth wide open, staring into the mirror, smearing lipstick over her childlike lips, as I sat daydreaming into the sweat rolling down my palms, phasing from one reality to another.

'Now drink it" I commanded. Kane gave no further thought and began to drink what he could in-between each whimpering quiver of repulsion. I felt dark, like light itself was suppressed, like the wrath of a deity was me, I was God! He then finished and looked up to me in waiting as I granted my conclusion - 'You don't know me, and you'll never find me - but know this: right here, right now, I own you. I own every inch of you, and I will leave you here with a smile on my smug undeserving face in that knowing, and every time from now on when you look at your pathetic self in the mirror, vision this moment, vision my face, when you belonged to me, when what is me, what I am! - Is inside you, and above all, remember that I am better than you!"

'Are you sure you don't mind me going out — you always seem off with me when I do?" — She paused, seeking reassurance, with an expression of sincerity clashed with a stance of frustration.
"Of course, I don't mind"
I replied,
I smiled.

I did mind, I did mind...

THE MEANING OF LIFE IS TO SUSTAIN EXISTENCE.

THE MEANING OF LIFE IS TO SUSTAIN EXISTENCE
BY MEANS OF CONSCIENCE.

THE MEANING OF LIFE IS TO SUSTAIN THE EXISTENCE
OF YOUR REALITY BY MEANS OF CONSCIENCE.

THE MEANING OF LIFE IS TO SUSTAIN THE EXISTENCE
OF REALITY BY MEANS OF CONSCIOUSNESS.

THE MEANING OF LIFE IS TO SUSTAIN THE EXISTENCE
OF REALITY BY MEANS OF OBSERVATION.

THE MEANING OF LIFE IS TO SUSTAIN THE EXISTENCE
OF REALITY.

THE MEANING OF LIFE IS TO SUSTAIN THE EXISTENCE.

THE MEANING OF LIFE IS TO SUSTAIN.

LIFE IS SUSTAIN.

REALITY IS EXISTENCE.

EXISTENCE IS NOT REALITY.

CHAPTER EIGHT

The meaning of life is to sustain the existence of reality by means of consciousness - for reality is an abstract until sustained by the sensors that react to the simulation that is reality. Time. Time is the rhythm of motion, motion is transition, from translation, it exists because it existed, but it only existed because it exists.

I exist — I am existing —
In much the way that a man holding onto a rope is flying.

I sat in a dreary cafe, full of filth, grime, and vulgar characters. My burnt breakfast was before me, on a plate, just looking at me, with murderous contempt.

"Please don't kill me!" - screeched in trepidation, a cry for solicited liberation from Kane's capturing clutches. Her body restricted, restrained, and pinned to the tiled floor as he hacked away at her hair, handful by handful.

"Look daddy! Look what I did in school today." The dad sat on the couch, staring straight ahead, his expression highlighted only by the flickering waves of light from the television screen. He had an expression of disgust: he always had an expression of disgust whenever the boy was around. The boy was stupid, and a burden to everyone that had the misfortune to be infected by his presence.

I paid the unmerited payment that was required to leave the cafe. I left. I walked. It rained. It always rained.

"See who'll want you now you slut!" - He spat - almost drooling with indignation. She felt each reverberated stride of crunch as handfuls of hair resided beside her. She heard each crisp strand of hair snip as she shut her eyes. She then felt nothing, nothing at all. What few tears she had left to will ran down the canal of the side of her eyes, past her ears, and soaked into the remaining hair she still had the privilege to possess.

"Look mummy! Look what I did in school today." The mother sat at the dining table, cold cup of tea before her, just staring at it. Her expression highlighted only by the waves of light that dashed across the room from the passing headlights of the vehicles that passed just outside. She looked sad: she always looked sad whenever the boy was around. The boy was annoying, and a burden to everyone that had the misfortune to be infected by his presence.

"Why don't you want me?!" He cried, indulged in his liberating torture as he gripped her wrists with one hand, and with the remainder held scissors to her stomach. Robyn tortured herself with numerous unpleasant scenarios that were leaping for attention in her head, when suddenly I walked down the street: people passed me, looking at me like I was in their way, like my presence brought nothing but burden to their day. She felt her jeans loosen to a snip, and with further snips of the scissors came the clarity of his motive. She heard a loosened belt buckle crash to the floor, but it wasn't her own. She knew what was coming, she knew she couldn't stop it, she knew it didn't matter, she knew he still wanted her.

"Are you OK?" enquired Colin, packed lunch in hand, and a deluded look of acceptance littering what area of his face was still distinguishable between each flabby curl that bordered around his smile in waves. The remaining one-way conversing that took place that day is not present in my memory; he filtered out from my attention. My attention instead was attracted to a strange man-shaped shadow that appeared seated at another table in the canteen. Suddenly he stopped, then pointed the now closed scissors to her face in a peaceful gesture of threat. I came to a decrepit shop that contained much reminiscent fancies that fancy exploration I did. Soon fancy became indulgence. A shadow filled with blackness so black that light itself was devoured through what was like a crack in reality to the corner of the canteen. A familiarity was lingering but an absolute did not present itself at the time, thus I rejected acknowledgment and removed my notebook from my pocket and began to study what I could study about the implausible events that lead to Robyn's return or be it, mine. Her toned trembling stomach exposed, her perfect skin excited him as her parting jeans exposed tease by tease her smooth recently shaved.

"I want you to leave" he commanded with reservation; she could read he was broken with discomfort. He always had issues with controlling his anger, and she being his most precious possession, he felt he didn't deserve her, and so would punish her for her obedience. It was because of this justification that she forgave, but he didn't stop. - to accept her right was to accept his wrong. Events continued to jump from one to another without transition. Time did not pass like it once did; when the clocks ticked from one second to the next, that silent moment of processing in-between each tick and tock had been removed. My life was not lived to make memories, but presented as memories, and more disturbingly, whatever time is now, consequently, I had less of it to experience, and less of it to control.

"Get out!" He commanded with a voice of domination.

She accepted his wish respectfully, picked up her hair, placed it in the bin, and as she walked away. There it was, no poetic foyer, no tear-jerking soundtrack to convey a rapture, just sat there, emerged in its own insignificance, a butterfly, a small gold butterfly, wings fringed with a wide earthly brown and a distinctive black and white eyespot on each, pinned to a small board, enclosed in a display box and labelled 'Gatekeeper'. There it was,

documented, owned, and dead!

The corkscrew of mind is a logic of the blind, tis a dream of a nightmare you follow resigned, and before the harvest of pass can sow its pace, you've lost a need, you've lost a place, for hearts of stone will ring no bell, when you're alone with no one to tell. Do you notice the stars that litter above? - It's like a wash of death that's splattered with love.

CHAPTER NINE

The bells sing to the rhythm of a diamond ring, there is a king for every string, like a bite for every sting, in vibration they gorged.

No monster is born but forged.

THE DELUSION OF LOVE GUTTED ME WITH ITS BLUNTED BLADE AND DISCARDED MY ENTRAILS ACROSS THE CHOPPING BOARD OF LIFE. EVERYTHING IS JUSTIFIABLE IN THIS BLINDNESS FOR COMFORT — THE ENTRAPMENT, LIKE A SACRIFICE TO A GOD, ALAS, LOVE IS TIMING — THE SOCIAL CONVENIENCE MET BY MUTUAL AGREEMENT THROUGH THE CRACK OF CHANCE, OR CHANCE OF WHAT COULD BE, IF WHAT WAS IS, AND THUS, WHAT WILL PASS IF NOT ALREADY LOST TO THE FORFEIT OF WHAT IS BUT FEAR. A WOMAN APPROACHED HIM, HE TRIED A TOKEN OF RELATION: A SMILE, A SPLINTERED EXCLAMATION OF A BLANK SHOT, SMILE BACK SHE DID NOT. LITTLE EVIDENCE HELD MY SUSPICION TO VALUE: HOWEVER, VALUE WAS NOW NOTHING BUT A SMUDGE OF WHITE NOISE — THE SOUNDTRACK TO HER DEFENCES. I TURN MY COLLAR. I COULD HEAR HER SLIPPERS DRAGGING ACROSS CARPETED FLOOR AS SHE APPROACHED THE ROOM: LIGHT THAT HAD ONCE BORDERED THE DOOR WAS SOON CHOKED AS SHE ENTERED. I RAN MY FINGERS ROUND HER FACE, EMBRACING HER BEAUTY, BEFORE COMBING MY FINGERS THROUGH HER HAIR. I'D PULL, FORCEFULLY AS I BEGAN TO BITE HER LIPS. SHE TILTED BACK IN SUBMISSION AND OPENED HER LIPS TO ME IN WANT. TIME DID NOT PASS LIKE IT ONCE DID. I THEN KISSED DOWN HER NECK - WHERE THE CLOCKS TICKED FROM ONE SECOND TO THE NEXT. TIME DID NOT PASS LIKE IT ONCE DID. SHE WAS LOOKING AT HER PHONE AGAIN: SHE WAS ALWAYS LOOKING AT HER PHONE, TAPPING AWAY, I KNEW NOT TO WHOM SHE TAPPED. SHE LIKED TO SOCIALISE BEHIND A PERSONALITY SHE MANUFACTURED USING PARTS SHE COLLECTED. I COULDN'T BE LIKE KANE: I COULDN'T TRAP HER. BUT EVERY TICK OF A CLOCK SHE FLUTTERED A LITTLE FURTHER AWAY.

She groaned as she dug her nails into my sides. I stopped. I tilted my head forward, staring provocatively at her with such licentious rapist want. She bit her voluptuous lip, she wasn't going to fight. I ripped her shirt open and began to kiss her vigorously all over her exposed. The club closed two hours before you called to be picked up!" Robyn gave no response, shifting her eyes side to side like she was scanning a book of blank pages for relevancy. Time did not pass like it once did: that silent moment of processing in-between each tick and tock had been removed, where the clocks ticked from one second to the next, time did not pass like it once did. Kane's erect fist ploughed Robyn's biddable slender figure to a longing quiver of reverberations, each throbbing thought of ebullient suspicion drove him mad. It was a conviction in gut, this scarcely even tangible nibble on the crust of one's disposition. She was cheating on me, and with that, the butterfly was sucked down the barrel of a vacuum cleaner, and into a past I had saved her from. Kane! Palpably evident, an inexpressible shame was masquerading blindly as stupor, for no confirmation is louder than silence. Don't let him get away" he heard commanded by the eldest as the group disappeared into the distance of the corridor. The small boy hid himself locked in a toilet cubicle, holding onto his recently severed hair. My life was not lived to make memories, but presented as memories, and more disturbingly... my life was not lived to make memories.

"Where were you last night?"
She stood there, scratching the side of her thumb, looking to her feet, staring at
her shoe, willing one to untie for distraction.

Yv mru mru crcru rdt yi mru mru jqud yi mfrcbt crjuh dej, rky crcru yi yi rij yi yi yi rdt mru Y'lu dem vehwej

After a series of suicide attempts, he reinvented himself a new personality, executed the old one, along with all associated memories. She ran her fingers into my hair, clasped, and then pressed me against her warm body. Everything she ever said was a lie, upon a pasty face of flab laid her fat eyes that held an ocean of deception. Up her legs I ran, almost scratching, my fingers assurgent, lifting her skirt on route. I dug my nails into her hips before sliding her knickers down. He destroyed everything he owned apart from a toy car and a novelty Christmas badge that he kept in a tin on his desk, but it terrified him that one day he would remember. Whatever time is now, consequently, it was presented as memories, and I had less of it to experience, and more disturbingly, less of it to control.

She was so annoying, bouncing around like a flea, constantly in my face, constantly asking and poking me, her stupid child voice squeaking — "What's up?" She'd get so moody when I disclosed nothing but a shrug, a fake smile, for a fake concern. She had become tainted. The world is laughing at me - every voice that had belittled me relentlessly was now roaring with laughter. I was tormented by

haunting thoughts of rivers of countless men touching her, speaking words only I could mean, fulfilling her want with smears of forged tokens.

I loved her, only me.

When he sees people that he recognises from his past, he feels like he's being dragged back into a plughole, but he doesn't think he is running away from an event or a person, more a memory of who he was. He would just sit there, staring, like he was studying the anatomy of his burnt English breakfast — every day he did this, every day he ordered it, but he never ate it.

Your brain is like a computer — a reaction to switches, a web of reactions, thoughts, and choices mapped like a set of algorithms of post-determined reactions, overlaying further sets of algorithms you've forged in learning. Did she think I did not know? I knew her plot, her motive. She was perpetually so desperate in craving for attention: she'd forge a fancy to make you fall in love with her. I spun her around, pushed her over the table, and then I took her, clawing her back in want. Soon apparent did it become that if you stop feeding her attention: she was back into Kane's arms. She never loved me: she just loved me loving her. I took her so hard she barely had time to gasp as she me immersed deep within her. I grabbed her shoulders and pulled her towards me. His name makes him sick, looking in the mirror makes him sick, and every time he thinks about his younger self he wants to kill him, and he's never wanted to kill anyone, but him, he'd happily torture him to an inch of his pathetic life. I knew she was cheating on me: I knew it was with Kane. Time did not pass like it once did. Like a trail on a window following a droplet of water still crashing downwards -reality applied only to the present and was changing with every fraction of motion. Palpably evident an inexpressible shame was masquerading blindly as stupor, for no confirmation is louder than silence. Whatever me is, it is the result of my environment, therefore Guilt… lays on the blooded hands of the functions. He would just sit there, staring, like he was studying the anatomy of his English breakfast — every day he did this, every day he ordered it, but he never ate. For his disposition was to equal value, and thus merited an equal fate.

CHAPTER ONE

The requiem of myself was furnished in the discolouring of my fingers from the ashes that were the remains of a moon that spun no more. The darkness cloaked, the silence choked, as rock became ice, no more sugar, no more spice. Nightmares would splice to the mercy of love's dice — there was no more sunshine to bathe my skin, as thin became the heart within. The whispers of dreams that scratched my skin soon became a butterfly under a pin. As the glass eye stares at the door, the heartbeat here nevermore, for as it drowned within a flood, consisting of its own bitter blood, like dreams deep in the scarring mud, tomorrow not cometh but a singular thud. "What the fuck is that?"

Kane barks at a mark on Robyn's neck. Robyn remained forcefully fixated on a blot apparent under the thin layer of paint that feebly coated the skirting board. When you're ok, but you're lying, singing but you're crying, sleeping but you're buying some more time. Don't let him get away" he heard commanded by the eldest as the group disappeared into the deep of the woods. The boy ran: he ran and never stopped running. Her wrists cuffed to the bed posts, blindfolded, and quivering with acute surges of want as I toyed with her, taunting her skin with the faintest touch, as I ran my finger all over her defenceless body - feeling, admiring her every curve, dip and every goosebump dimple that coated her perfect tight skin.

When you're busy, but you're trying, silent but you're replying, laughing but you're dying, one more time.

"It's nothing — just nothing" She replied with little time to fabricate much more whilst covering her mark with her palm. Her face layered with guilt but coated with fear as she retreated towards the bedroom, "I need to sleep." Kane couldn't understand - why would she cheat on him, why would she want to leave him? He's obsessive and hypersensitive. He won't interact with the other children: he just sits there, stroking things.

"Got you!" exclaimed a gang member, vulnerably restrained he stood. They fenced him, taunting him, for finally they had him, and he was going nowhere. Kane seized her wrist: "I'm not done" he said in lifeless tone that sparked a trembling in trepidation throughout Robyn. The shadows of the gang members and the towering trees that surrounded united as he cowered to a ball. Two of four boys grabbed the small boy by his arms and proceeded to tie him to a tree. The boy struggled and begged: but realised he was merely paying kindle to their amusement, and thus he stopped.

"I can't take it anymore!" She broke down crying, as she reassigned the blame of her actions in an unconvinced fashion with every look and glance fixated on everything but him. "What is wrong with you?" Kane's disquieting serenity grew with his anger as he feasted on his incurable vice -

"Let's cut off his willy!" proposed one of the gang members with a joyful flick of his lip.

"Yeah!" favours the eldest, as he revealed the possession of a knife. He held it like it was charmed as he examined the perfection of the blade in reverence. They pulled the boy's trousers down, with their inclination inspired by every scream.

He held the knife to him with pause, savouring every moment. I kissed her chained wrists and slowly move across to her collarbone, down the side of her perfectly smooth, naked slender body, nibbling her hips, pressing on her groin, coaxing her, her yearn, her burn.

"Hold on", says the eldest as he began to unzip his trousers. The splinters of discomfort prevailed by loyalty. "Open your mouth and we'll spare your tinky winky" he commanded, moving toward the boy.

'You can beat me all you like — I no longer feel it' She spoke with misinformed confidence, but without a glance to her eye he grabbed her by the wrist and dragged her away from the room. She found herself flung into the kitchen. The gang rejoiced in a unity of hysterics that fuelled the leader to urinate with their approval. The boy struggled for breath; he began to choke but his mouth remained open. Kane grabbed a knife from the kitchen drawer.

'What? You going to kill me? — I'm already dead!' she whimpered.

'Why are you doing this?' she demanded but he didn't respond, he just continued to examine the perfection of the blade in reverence.

'As you were such a good boy, we will spare your little maggot there and instead... simply remove your fingers' The rushed eagerness disturbed the boy, no spark of hope for him was present.

'I'm not going to kill you Robyn' He spoke with a delicate tongue. The words alone were foreplay to him, mocking her with his excitement for an action that was soon to pass in revulsion for her. He grabbed her right hand, slammed it flat to the chopping board. The eldest took the knife to the boy's fingers, the true horror of what was to come soon dawned on the boy, but whimper a word he could not, for even fear had disowned him in fear as he looked on in dismay as his torturer toyed the blade around each individual finger. The true horror of what was to come soon dawned on Robyn but whimper a word she could not, even fear had disowned her in fear as she looked on in dismay. He savoured every moment as he positioned her fingers with precision.

She was so beautiful. She was the sunshine that smacked the moon across the face and showed him the beauty of world he had always looked away from. She was the only person that could see him, she was the only person that could hear him. She was the warmth in a world of ice. She was the only key in existence that fitted the lock to a world that only they could go. She was friend, she was love, but she's not there now, because this body before me can't be her. I continued kissing up the inside of her thighs, teasing her, welcomed in gasp as she arched her back in beckoning need.

She would have fought; she would have never given up. No matter how far away we drifted. We both would have sooner died holding hands than let one of us go. She's not her, I don't know who she is, but I hope that my Robyn never returns, because it would kill her to see what had become of her, of us, and what had become of me.

Without jest came a reverberated slam! She froze in disbelief as she stared at her now severed fingers, fingers she'd had all her life, just lying there, detached, no longer hers. She didn't look in pain, she didn't look in the state of any emotion despite every emotion flooding through her and tearing her within. Her open, wanting, needing, craving with every scratching need in her pathetic quivering body. I took her in assault. I couldn't stop staring: her eyes that held an ocean of deception drowned me in fear, in jealousy, in hatred. She looked so broken: holding a towel around her hand, staring at me like she didn't know who I was anymore. My knife held out, now sliding, slowly into her stomach. She didn't even move, she didn't even whimper, like she couldn't feel a thing. I felt like she was lost, she was gone: a thousand miles away and yet, as my blade slowly penetrated her, I had never felt so close to her as I watched the sparkle in her eye die, and in it - did I. Our eyes never parted until she collided with the floor, her corpse now moving no more.

Something horrible happened when I was younger, a horror that I cannot live with. So, I dealt with this by creating a 'new me' within myself. I created a new personality, and everything that could be linked to the old me was cut out, my possessions, my taste in music, in film, my hobbies, my friends. Suppressed reminiscences became the window for my obsessions of time, with fractions of subtractions that echoed in rhyme. Time did not pass like it once did. Kane stumbled to the bed, emotionless if not for the clink of a knocked glass: a small flood of water on the carpet became a flood of despair as the water soaked into the carpet like the fading of a veil. An inner quiver shredded me from within as the true horror of truth sliced through me like a blunt blade hacking through the corpse of cause — and in that — I passed out. The only word that will suffice is a scream, in this broken world it would seem - a dream

I then fantasised about the old pathetic me being murdered: I would often fantasise graphically about killing the old me myself. But I was open, as open as a book, just with a few pages torn out. "Are you OK?" Life was presented as memories — because that's all they were. I'm nothing but a footprint, a mere inch deep in snow. Did she know, with her transition in decay, festering in the trivial shadow of a shadow, she's not who she was, yesterday? Time is a measurement that only exists in the confinement of our dimension. "I'm going to hug you" English breakfast before me, with little to no desire to consume it as it festers before me, in a defiance of purpose. Look at her, just lying there two-tone. Soon she'll turn putrid, good for nothing but a feast for maggots. How dare you judge me! I'm going to be a supernova! And with each phantom breeze that donated a splinter of seductive tease. I loathed the old me with unmeasurable hatred, for reasons I believe was to assist in my dissociation.

"Why are you doing this?" Look at you, just lying there, digesting your own intestines, eyes will bulge, tongue will swell, your own skin will reject you as your bones disperse. Your existence be in my mind now, and in my death be yours. You did this! Whilst the rest of us like moths flying pitifully to the light, you casted a shadow, a shadow that devoured what remained of the world. Whilst slivering shadows waltzed on their toes across the sharp forms of the room. Even a child with a pocket full of chocolate stars can tell you - nothing is great if something is greater. You were the blizzard that tore reality. Each form of surface bringing birth to alternative forms of light that sparkled like stars drowning in a lake. I reinvented myself, I cut off all ties to my past. That child is dead, I am dead. She moved in. All her stuff was already in my home. She returned.

THE PHILOSOPHICAL AFTERBIRTH OF A LIFE YOU SUBMERGED IN A JAR OF PRESERVE

I never again disclosed the memories, even to myself. I cut away anybody or anything that related to that memory. For whilst no memory is held of it, by me or anybody else, the existence of that reality becomes dismissible. 'Your eyes change' the beauty of this seclusion laid tinted only by the dishonesty that befell a lifetime in discomfort. From a time I no longer hold as my own, I cut it out. 'We've been together for two years now, why do you look at me like you don't know me?' There came the sobbing of a small boy slumped to a chair in the corner — he stole my face, my evil dead face. My limp and lifeless body burdened no more by a retarded, rejected, pathetic lump of unlovable piece of hideous long tormented faces, grey, judging me. Upon further focus soon came the submission of dismay, why my guilt dared not cross path with my thoughts. Motion is a straight line that can be drawn as a dot, there is no time for time.

'You're a nice person really.' I was in and out of moments like blots of ink on water, repeatedly doodling the figure of eight on the cover of my notebook. I could vision myself rip open further away the skin, through the membrane, and cracking, like an eggshell, inverting myself - freeing myself. But it is always there, whilst I am dancing in ignorance, it is there. I can feel its presence, like a reality I am ignoring, just ticking away, in the background. Like my corpse is just right there, all this time, under the floorboards below where I stand, waiting patiently. 'Don't you remember?' For hidden from the reality in denial, was a boy tearing out lump by lump his own internal organs. I looked to the floor, there lay all my hopes and dreams, there lay nothing more. She was the only person that could see me: she was the only person that could hear me. She lied to me: everything was an act all along. With a sobbing that indicated not despair, but despair in lacking. Down a country road I drive, I drive so fast. As each meaningless organ greeted the floor with such casual insignificance. Evil is more than just a relative concept, it is an energy: it can't be created, it can't be destroyed, it can only be transferred. So very fast I drive.

Why do you always act like you don't remember?" I release my grip from the steering wheel, to release myself from the guilt of suicide I leave it to fate. She welcomed in gasp as she arched her back in beckoning need, she desired to be pinned, and judging by the gratefully damaged look in her eyes, she expected differently. I kicked her out, enough was enough.

Honestly it's like living with two different people sometimes." I caught a butterfly, he exclaimed with joy. For everything I have done and everything I will do, everything that I would regard as me, in whatever part of me is me. Capture it I did, and now it belonged to him. I then stopped sobbing to turn and look at me, a pause that granted my hollow eyes the power to paralyse me in fear. Every thought, every action, everything was created by everything outside of me to the extent that there is no me left.

But it is always there, whilst I am dancing in ignorance, it is there. I can feel its presence, like a reality I am ignoring, just ticking away, in the background. Like my corpse is just right there, all this time, under the floorboards below where I stand, waiting patiently.

"Well? What are you waiting for?" Maggots now swim in the pus of the festered blisters they formed. I am a mere sack of reactions. I screamed a scream that only an animal could rally, so emotionally raw in emotionless emotion. The one solid holding in consciousness of I think therefore I am is nothing but just another delusion. I do not think, I react.

Kane had never left his room, the events that proceeded where merely events of a prior overcrowding. The mere act of pondering is nothing but a predetermined response. I find myself much older now, and I'm sorry. I am sorry I murdered the old me, his innocence gutted out to give way to this 'new me', this dead-inside shadow, like a fictional character who was created, not born, with all my fake interests and dreams, my fake quirks and traits. Like Frankenstein's Monster, I am nothing but a conception of what I killed. It burrowed within my reflexes, time is just two parallel lines overlapping in memories, because there never was a Kane, I was Kane — I am Kane, he was me — he was always me - everything was me.

Printed in Great Britain
by Amazon

26721589R00078